SPOTLIGHT ON GLOBAL ISSUES

EQUALITY AND SOCIAL JUSTICE

Rachael Morlock

ROSEN PUBLISHING

NEW YORK

Published in 2022 by The Rosen Publishing Group, Inc.
29 East 21st Street, New York, NY 10010

Copyright © 2022 by The Rosen Publishing Group, Inc.

All rights reserved. No part of this book may be reproduced in any form without permission in writing from the publisher, except by a reviewer.

First Edition

Editor: Theresa Emminizer
Book Design: Michael Flynn

Photo Credits: Cover, p. 12 Jacob Lund/Shutterstock.com; (series globe background) photastic/Shutterstock.com; p. 5 Anderson Ross Photography Inc/DigitalVision/Getty Images; p. 6 https://commons.wikimedia.org/wiki/File:Declaration_of_Independence_(1819),_by_John_Trumbull.jpg; p. 7 Hulton Archive/Getty Images; p. 8 Stringer/AFP/Getty Images; p. 9 https://commons.wikimedia.org/w/index.php?title=File:Eleanor_Roosevelt_UDHR.jpg&oldid=387677480; p. 11 -/Stringer/AFP/Getty Images; p. 13 Bryan R. Smith/AFP/Getty Images; p. 14 Bloomberg/Getty Images; p. 15 Cole Bennetts/Getty Images; p. 17 Rawpixel.com/Shutterstock.com; p. 18 Buyenlarge/Archive Photos/Getty Images; p. 19 Joseph Sohm/Shutterstock.com; p. 20 Kobby Dagan/Shutterstock.com; p. 21 Salvatore Di Nofi/Keystone/AP Images; p. 23 The Washington Post/Getty Images; p. 24 Barcroft Media/Getty Images; p. 25 Manish Swarup/AP/Getty Images; p. 26 fotosparrow/Shutterstock.com; p. 27 Gopen Rai/AFP/Getty Images; p. 29 Sia Kambou/AFP/Getty Images.

Cataloging-in-Publication Data

Names: Morlock, Rachael.
Title: Equality and social justice / Rachael Morlock.
Description: New York : Rosen Publishing, 2022. | Series: Spotlight on global issues | Includes glossary and index.
Identifiers: ISBN 9781725323346 (pbk.) | ISBN 9781725323377 (library bound) | ISBN 9781725323353 (6 pack)
Subjects: LCSH: Equality--Juvenile literature. | Social justice--Juvenile literature.
Classification: LCC HM821.M667 2022 | DDC 305--dc23

Manufactured in the United States of America

Some of the images in this book illustrate individuals who are models. The depictions do not imply actual situations or events.

CPSIA Compliance Information: Batch #CSR22. For further information contact Rosen Publishing, New York, New York at 1-800-237-9932.

CONTENTS

DEFENDING RIGHTS 4
GENDER EQUALITY 10
LGBTQ RIGHTS 14
PEOPLE OF THE WORLD 16
RACIAL DISCRIMINATION 18
RELIGIOUS FREEDOM 22
JUSTICE FOR MIGRANTS 24
EQUALITY FOR DISABLED PEOPLE 26
SUSTAINABLE DEVELOPMENT 28
VOICES FOR EQUALITY 30
GLOSSARY 31
INDEX 32
PRIMARY SOURCE LIST 32
WEBSITES 32

CHAPTER ONE
DEFENDING RIGHTS

The ways resources, opportunities, and privileges are distributed in a society shows how fair or just that society is. But what is fair and just? This type of discussion usually focuses on three main terms—equality, equity, and social justice.

Equality means providing the same rights and opportunities to everyone. The civil rights movement in the United States is a historic example of the struggle for equality in America. In an era of segregation, African Americans called attention to the unjust laws that prevented them from voting and being equal members of society. The United States took an important step toward equality by protecting these rights with new laws.

Equality often includes the idea of equity. Instead of equal opportunities, equity refers to equal outcomes. It recognizes the role of privilege and relies on the idea that fairness is more than equal treatment. For example, the Americans with Disabilities Act became law in 1990. This act supports people with disabilities in accessing the same services and opportunities as other members of society. The requirement for accessible entrances on public buildings is just one example of equity in action. It takes into account different abilities and privileges in order to work toward an equal outcome.

Social justice puts equality and equity into action. It takes form through social, economic, and political policies that defend the rights of all members of society. Social justice focuses on equal rights and outcomes regardless of sex, race, ethnicity, religion, place of origin, disability, and economic status.

A trend toward social justice has slowly evolved through history. It began with the philosophical idea of equality long before it became a political goal. For most of human history, society has been organized with strict hierarchies of power. Ancient systems were based on the belief that some people were naturally better than others. They commanded greater power and greater resources.

It wasn't until the Enlightenment in the 17th and 18th century that the idea of equality gained global popularity. Philosophers such as John Locke and Jean-Jacques Rousseau thought of political structures as a social contract. They understood that the political power of rulers is granted through an unspoken agreement with their citizens, not through a divine or natural right. If the people within a society were unhappy with the social contract, then they had the power to change it. Immanuel Kant was another philosopher who promoted ideas of equality and the rights of citizens.

SIGNING OF THE DECLARATION OF INDEPENDENCE

French revolutionaries stormed a military fort—a symbol of the monarchy's power—on Bastille Day in 1789. Like the French and American revolutions, many movements for political equality have been violent.

People put these ideas into motion in the 18th century. Revolutionary movements in the United States and France produced the U.S. Declaration of Independence in 1776 and the French Declaration of the Rights of Men and of the Citizen in 1789. Both documents mention the natural equality of all citizens and the importance of individual rights. In the 19th century, more nations became involved in independence movements to throw off the restraints of colonial powers and gain greater rights for citizens. The ideals of democracy and equality took root in cultures around the world.

The march toward social justice gained momentum after the Industrial Revolution. During this period, which stretched from about 1750 to about 1850, a large portion of the world's population shifted from farm work to industry. People created new technologies and factories for creating goods. Within these industries, owners treated and paid workers poorly. Inequalities between social classes deepened.

The injustices of industrialization sparked new movements and laws to make life more equitable. In the Progressive Era of the 19th century, reformers pushed for laws that would improve working conditions, housing situations, and general quality of life for the poorest members of society. Other reforms grew out of the movement in order to address issues of inequality between sexes, races, and ethnicities. These movements affected world governments and encouraged them to recognize the rights of all their citizens.

ASSEMBLY OF UNITED NATIONS, 1948

Eleanor Roosevelt, the former First Lady of the United States, inspects the Universal Declaration of Human Rights. Mrs. Roosevelt was a member of the UN committee that wrote it.

The next global milestone in the history of equality and social justice came about after World War II. The horrors and injustices of the war inspired world leaders to form the United Nations (UN) to organize global peace efforts. In 1948, the UN adopted the Universal Declaration of Human Rights. This listed the fundamental rights of all people around the world.

Today, 192 nations have signed the UN declaration. However, many people still face discrimination and injustice. Because of aspects of their identity, they're prevented from accessing rights, services, opportunities, and resources. Unequal treatment often relates to the gender, sexual orientation, race, ethnicity, religion, place of origin, disability, or economic status of individuals and communities.

CHAPTER TWO
GENDER EQUALITY

The Universal Declaration of Human Rights claims that a person's gender shouldn't interfere with their ability to access resources and opportunities. But more than 70 years later, this isn't a reality. The struggle for gender equality has chiefly focused on women's rights. In most societies throughout world history, men have held greater rights. They've been the primary decision-makers whose choices and policies have shaped the lives of women.

In 1792, a British woman named Mary Wollstonecraft wrote *A Vindication of the Rights of Woman*. This work argued for the equal treatment of women politically, socially, and economically. Following in Wollstonecraft's footsteps, female leaders of the 19th century lobbied for greater rights. However, they became increasingly aware of their limited ability to change society.

In many countries, women were born with very few rights, and many women lost their rights when they married. Even in democracies, women were second-class citizens who couldn't vote. They couldn't become lawmakers, and they had no voice in their own governments.

In response, women's suffrage, or right to vote, movements swept across the globe. New Zealand, Australia, Finland, and Norway were the first countries to grant women suffrage. After World War I, 28 other countries gave voting rights to women, and more followed after World War II. Suffrage campaigns represent some of the most important social justice movements of the 20th century. They've resulted in the inclusion of women in governments around the world as lawmakers and leaders. Still, women are outnumbered by men in political positions.

New Zealand (then a self-governing colony) recognized women's right to vote in 1893. In Saudi Arabia, shown here, women were able to vote for the first time in 2015.

Although the right to vote has granted greater political **power**, **women** and girls continue to face discrimination. Even when laws protect women's rights, social attitudes can threaten them. Many **campaigns** to achieve equality for girls and women focus on **education**, **health** care, economic equality, and violence against women.

Educating girls is a powerful tool for improving **women's** lives. It can reduce the incidence of child marriage for girls, increase the income earned by women, and make the communities and countries they live in more stable. However, girls are more likely than boys to never **attend** school. About 132 million **girls** around the world are currently out of school. For gender equality to exist, boys and girls need equal access to quality schools.

Memory Banda, right, was 13 when she took a stand against child marriage in Malawi. She's shown here at the Clinton Global Initiative in 2016. Child marriage can lead to poverty, health problems, and a lack of education for girls.

Closing the gap between men and women's wages is another gender equality goal. Men generally make more money than women, even when they perform the same work. Around the world, the **average** woman makes about 77 cents for every dollar a man makes. Low **wages** prevent women from acquiring necessities such as education, health care, and nutritious foods.

Calling attention to **gender equality** problems is an important step in fixing them. Once a problem is seen and understood, then communities can take action. In Malawi, Memory Banda convinced her village to end cultural practices that hurt girls after her 11-year-old sister was forced to marry. Her story and activism influenced **many** others, and in 2017, Malawi outlawed child marriage. Banda **and others** continue to **fight** for an end to child **marriage** worldwide.

CHAPTER THREE

LGBTQ RIGHTS

Beyond women's rights, gender equality includes a focus on the lesbian, gay, bisexual, transgender, and queer (LGBTQ) community. Gender is the word used for sets of social expectations about how men and women should behave. People who fall outside established social categories can be targeted by discriminatory laws and practices. One goal of LGBTQ activists is to expand social categories so that people of all sexual orientations and gender identities are recognized.

Social justice movements for the LGBTQ community aim to end discrimination. Over one-third of the world's countries criminalize LGBTQ behavior. That means that people can be arrested, punished, and jailed because of whom they love. In seven of these countries, LGBTQ people can be put to death because of their sexual identity. In other countries, laws protect LGBTQ communities, but social attitudes cause violence and discrimination.

In movements around the world, the rainbow flag is a symbol of LGBTQ pride. An activist waves the flag in 2017 to support the legalization of same-sex marriage in Australia.

LGBTQ people around the world suffer from unequal housing, education, employment, and health-care rights. Activists are working on changing the laws and institutional structures that exclude LGBTQ people. They provide training, work to elect leaders who value the LGBTQ community, and speak out against the violence that threatens LGBTQ individuals and communities.

In June 2016, the UN Human Rights council adopted a new resolution to oppose violence and discrimination against LGBTQ people. Since then, India, Angola, Botswana, and Trinidad and Tobago have decriminalized same-sex relationships. The UN's Free and Equal campaign has used social media, events, and educational projects to bring attention to LGBTQ issues around the world and draw support from community members and allies.

CHAPTER FOUR
PEOPLE OF THE WORLD

Wherever you are, you're likely to see people who look physically different from you. Variations occur in skin color, hair texture, facial features, head shape, height, and more. People have a wide range of inherited physical traits that influence how they're identified.

For centuries, people with certain shared traits have been grouped together into races. The separation of races may appear scientific, but it's actually a form of social categorization. That's because people are divided into races based on biological traits, such as skin color, that societies decided are important. These traits aren't important in and of themselves.

There is no single definition of race, and regions of the world recognize different racial categories. Races are difficult to pin down because all humans are very similar. Physical traits and lines of descent overlap in so many ways that groups of people, no matter where they're from in the world or how they look, are more alike than different.

Advances in technology have proven these similarities by making it possible to study the genetic makeup of humankind. The Human Genome Project was a global partnership between biologists, physicists, chemists, and engineers to map human genes using the DNA of people from around the world. Launched in 1990 and completed in 2003, the Human Genome Project proved the genetic unity of humankind.

Unfortunately, race has been and is still used as a basis for denying rights. Racism is the idea that some races are better than others. This mindset has caused inequality and injustice throughout the world.

No matter what they look like, how they sound, or where they're from, the DNA of any two humans will always be at least 99.9 percent the same.

CHAPTER FIVE

RACIAL DISCRIMINATION

Race became an important political and social subject during the European conquest, a period when Europe conquered other nations. White Europeans drew distinctions between themselves and others. They developed a hierarchy that assigned certain characteristics and behaviors to different races. They used it to justify the conquering, enslavement, and segregation of large populations.

Discrimination against people of African descent has persisted long after the end of slavery. Two of the most notable global examples of racial discrimination happened through segregation in the United States and apartheid in South Africa. Both countries enforced strict separations between black and white citizens. In response, 20th century civil rights movements developed to demand equality. These movements were successful in creating stronger legal protections for black people. However, social and cultural biases still exist around the world and cause racial discrimination.

Even after school segregation was outlawed, African American students, like the boy shown here in 1956, faced harassment and discrimination from their white peers.

In the United States, racial gaps exist in income, housing, education, and employment. Black people often face barriers in taking out loans, buying houses, accessing health care, attending college, and getting hired. They are regularly treated with prejudice by the criminal justice system.

Black Lives Matter was created in 2014 to stand up to racism. It's now a global movement dedicated to ending violence against black people around the world. Similarly, Racism, It Stops With Me is a movement in Australia to combat racist attitudes and actions.

Racism targets more than black communities. Groups around the world experience its negative effects in different ways. No matter what race you identify with, establishing racial equality is everyone's responsibility.

Sometimes the term "race" is used broadly to talk about ethnicity or **nationality**. Like races, ethnicities are social categories that result in distinct groups of people. However, ethnicity refers to cultural **traits**. Heritage, language, religion, and traditions can all be cultural **elements** that make ethnic groups different from each other.

Ethnic groups come in a variety of sizes and **geographic ranges**. An ethnicity can include people of different nations and races. For instance, Hispanic ethnicity is extensive and has members in many nations united by language. At the same time, multiple ethnicities can exist within one country. For example, indigenous, or native, groups in Brazil make up less than 1 percent of the population, but they are divided into 230 different cultural groups and speak about 180 indigenous languages. They have their own ethnic identities that are distinct from each other and from other Brazilians.

Hamangaí Pataxó, shown here, is a young Brazilian who has been dedicated to protecting indigenous rights since she was a teenager. In 2019, she addressed the Young Activists Summit in Geneva, Switzerland.

Social justice depends on the equality of all people no matter their ethnicity, but ethnicity is often tied to injustice. Tensions between ethnic groups have historically led to slavery, segregation, genocide, and forced assimilation. Assimilation is the act or process of blending in with the customs of a group of people. Ethnic conflicts have occurred on every continent. They're still resulting in violence, discrimination, and displacement for millions of people.

To counteract inequality, individuals and governments can support ethnic minorities and help refugees fleeing ethnic conflicts. Multicultural societies are strongest when they embrace their many parts and celebrate differences. As an individual, showing respect for all ethnicities and treating everyone with dignity can go a long way toward achieving equality.

CHAPTER SIX
RELIGIOUS FREEDOM

The ability to practice your chosen religion is a fundamental freedom that's protected within the Universal Declaration of Human Rights. Over 84 percent of the world's population is part of a religious group, so religious freedom is widely important. However, many people are treated unfairly by their government, society, or both because of their beliefs.

Government restrictions on religious practices can take shape through laws, policies, and state or military actions. These include the ban on burkas in France and Saudi Arabian laws that make it illegal to practice non-Muslim religions in public. Social discrimination results from the actions of individuals or organized groups. Harassment and terrorist acts often target members of minority religions.

Around the world, 43 countries have state religions. Islam is the official religion of 27 countries, 13 countries are Christian, 2 are Buddhist, and 1 is Jewish. Where state religions are legally and socially favored, minority religions are at risk. Most governments with strong religious repression are in the Middle East and North Africa. However, religious restrictions are on the rise across the globe.

The UN has launched two recent programs to protect religious freedom in the world. The first project is aimed at opposing hate speech and promoting respect between religions. The second strives to protect holy sites and places of worship so that everyone can practice their religion peacefully. Educating people about different religions is another powerful way to encourage understanding and respect for all faiths.

Hana Kaur Mangat was 12 when she helped found Sikh Kid 2 Kid in Maryland. She led training sessions alongside other young Sikhs to help teach adult educators about her religion.

CHAPTER SEVEN

JUSTICE FOR MIGRANTS

The Universal Declaration of Human Rights mentions the protection of rights regardless of national origin. This is essential to people who must make their home in a new country. Whether they are migrants, immigrants, or refugees, 258 million people around the world live outside their country of origin.

Some people have left **willingly to search for better opportunities** or escape poverty. They may seek access to human **rights, such as clean** water, food, health care, and housing, that are unavailable in their home countries. About 65.3 million people, however, have been **forced to** leave their homes because of conflict, persecution, or disaster.

Protesters gather in Bangladesh to demand justice for climate refugees.

In September 2019, Ridhima Pandey joined 15 other young activists in suing five leading countries for contributing to climate change and failing to protect children from its effects.

Climate change is a significant force driving migration today. Unpredictable weather patterns, destructive storms, floods, long dry periods, and rising sea levels displace people as climate change grows and intensifies. The most vulnerable populations of the world are most heavily affected. Lack of infrastructure and dependence on stressed ecosystems make it difficult for poor communities to recover from extreme weather. People lose their homes, jobs, and safety because of climate change.

Ridhima Pandey has taken the issue of climate change to heart. The young teen lives in Uttarakhand, India, where floods and landslides have deadly effects. Pandey has also witnessed pollution and deforestation in India.

The climate justice movement recognizes the inequality of climate change. The communities that will be most impacted by climate change are those least responsible for causing it. Young people like Pandey push for renewable energy technologies and stricter global standards to protect the world they will inherit from adults.

CHAPTER EIGHT

EQUALITY FOR DISABLED PEOPLE

Around the world, people with disabilities have experienced inequality and been denied many basic human rights. About 15 percent of the world's population lives with a physical, mental, intellectual, or sensory disability. Since disabilities prevent many people from **working**, these people are twice as likely to live in poverty. Other **disadvantages** include unequal access to health care, housing, transportation, education, public services, and civic rights such as voting. People in this community frequently experience abuse, neglect, and exclusion.

Social justice movements for people with disabilities are **fairly new**. One movement first developed in the 1960s in the United States. Drawing on the tools of the civil rights movement, disability rights activists planned sit-ins, marches, and protests. One great **achievement** was the Americans with Disabilities Act of 1990, **which promised legal** protection, accessibility, and inclusion programs.

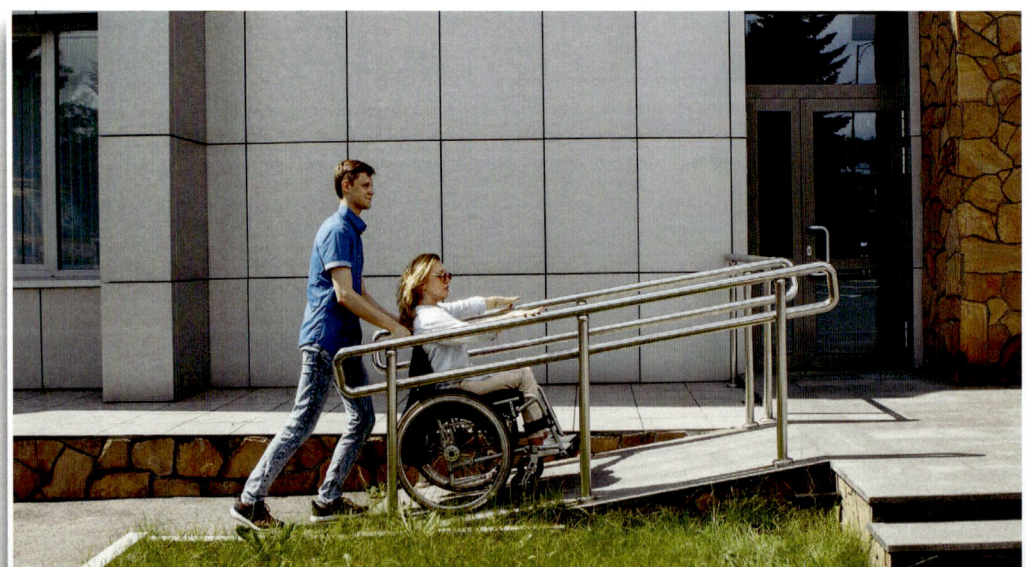

26

DisasterHack is a company that makes 3-D printed prosthetics for people injured in disasters. The company will donate this prosthetic hand to someone who couldn't afford it on their own.

On the world stage, people with disabilities received global support through the UN's Convention on the Rights of Persons with Disabilities. Member states agreed to advance and protect the rights of all people with disabilities in 2006. This was a show of support for 1 billion people worldwide with disabilities.

Technology has a large and exciting role in disability equality. As engineers develop many innovations, they create new opportunities for people to live and work independently. Technologies such as 3-D printed limbs can increase self-sufficiency. Smart glasses may help many of the 39 billion blind people in the world see contrasts in light. Other device-based technologies can help people with sensory disabilities communicate. Creative technologies can help people with disabilities be more independent and active.

CHAPTER NINE
SUSTAINABLE DEVELOPMENT

Inequality is present in all countries, from the least to the most developed. As a universal problem, it needs to be tackled on national, regional, and global levels in order to be solved. It's a broad issue with many complicated and interconnected parts that must all be addressed.

Economic inequality occurs on a dramatic scale. In terms of income, the bottom 50 percent of the population is responsible for less than 10 percent of the world's wealth. This gap is widening. It prevents overall economic growth and threatens global financial systems. It also poses the danger of social and political instability around the world.

Equality is essential for sustainable development. This is the idea that decisions and policies should equally consider the present and future. Sustainable development values long-term success over short-term benefits. Inequality has economic, social, and environmental effects within and between countries. All these concerns must be weighed as the international community decides how to combat inequality in a way that will have positive, long-term outcomes around the globe.

Inequality is most extreme in the Americas and least extreme in Scandinavia. Moving forward, the more successful Scandinavian models could influence global and national movements in reforming taxation and employment and offering strong social services such as accessible housing, advanced education, childcare, and health care. For many countries and international organizations, this may require a change in mindset. Instead of measuring progress by immediate economic boosts for the few, engaging and supporting the most vulnerable members of society must be the priority.

The world produces enough food to feed all of humankind, but one-third of this food is wasted and 800 million people are underfed. Sustainable equality movements must focus on effective food distribution.

CHAPTER TEN
VOICES FOR EQUALITY

Everyone has a role to play in making equality and social justice realities. Educating yourself about the multiple and layered issues of equality is a vital first step. It gives you the tools and information you need to ask important questions, find your voice, and speak out for change.

Actions for equality take place at all levels of society and politics. Start small in your own community by paying attention to inequality and listening to those most affected. Within your government, encourage leaders to adopt policies and laws that support and protect disadvantaged people. On a global scale, push for change by getting involved in UN or other international campaigns for equality. You can also tap in to social media and online communities that keep activists connected and united in their goals.

You can work for equality by standing up in everyday ways for people who are marginalized. Be an ally by stepping in when you see bullying and discrimination. Treat everyone with dignity and respect. Find mentors and stories that inspire you to learn and be more. These are powerful ways you can change your experiences and those of others and make the world more just.

All activists are ordinary people. They've chosen to put their energy and creativity into improving their world and the lives of others. You can make that choice too. If you feel passionate about the need for equality and social justice in the world, then challenge yourself to work for change in your own way.

GLOSSARY

activist (AK-tih-vist) Someone who acts strongly in support of or against an issue.

apartheid (uh-PAHR-tahyt) Racial segregation, or specifically, a former policy of separating and oppressing the nonwhite population in South Africa.

burka (BUR-kuh) A garment worn by some Muslim women that covers the entire body with a veiled opening for the eyes.

decriminalize (dee-KRI-muh-nuh-liyz) To remove laws against an activity.

discrimination (dih-skrih-muh-NAY-shun) Different—usually unfair—treatment based on factors such as a person's race, age, religion, or gender.

displacement (dis-PLAY-smuhnt) Movement out of a certain area.

ethnicity (eth-NIH-suh-tee) A group of people that share a common culture.

genetic (juh-NEH-tik) Referring to the parts of cells that control the appearance, growth, and other traits of a living thing.

genocide (JEH-nuh-siyd) The purposeful elimination of a national, racial, or cultural group of people.

genome (JEE-nohm) A full set of chromosomes that determine inheritable traits.

harassment (huh-RAS-muhnt) The act of creating a hostile or unpleasant situation for someone through unwanted contact.

hierarchy (HY-uh-rahr-kee) A ranking of some sort.

infrastructure (IN-fruh-struhk-chuhr) The equipment and structures needed for a country, state, or region to function properly.

marginalized (MAHRJ-nuh-liyzd) Placed in a position of powerlessness.

repression (rih-PREH-shuhn) The act or process of repressing, or keeping something down.

segregation (seh-grih-GAY-shuhn) The separation of people based on race, class, sex, gender, or ethnicity.

technology (tek-NAH-luh-jee) A method that uses science to solve problems and the tools used to solve those problems.

vulnerable (VUHL-nuh-ruh-buhl) Open to attack or harm.

INDEX

A
Americans with Disabilities Act, 4, 26
Angola, 15
Australia, 10, 15, 19

B
Banda, Memory, 13
Black Lives Matter, 19
Botswana, 15
Brazil, 20

F
Finland, 10
France, 22

I
India, 15, 25
Industrial Revolution, 8

L
LGBTQ community, 14, 15

M
Malawi, 13
Mangat, Hana Kaur, 23

N
New Zealand, 10, 11
Norway, 10

P
Pandey, Ridhima, 25
Pataxó, Hamangaí, 21
Progressive Era, 8

R
Racism, It Stops With Me, 19

S
Saudi Arabia, 11, 22
Scandinavia, 28
Sikh Kid 2 Kid, 23
South Africa, 18

T
Trinidad and Tobago, 15

U
United Nations (UN), 8, 9, 15, 22, 27, 30
United States, 4, 9, 18, 19, 26
Universal Declaration of Human Rights, 9, 10, 22, 24

W
World War I, 10
World War II, 9, 10

PRIMARY SOURCE LIST

Page 8
President of the Council Vincent Auriol delivers the opening speech at the third assembly of the United Nations, Paris. Photograph. September 22, 1948. Getty Images.

Page 9
Eleanor Roosevelt. Photograph. FPG/Staff. January 1, 1948. Getty Images.

Page 21
Activist Hamangaí Pataxó. Photograph. Salvatore Di Nolfe. December 10, 2019. Young Activists Summit in Geneva, Switzerland. Keystone via AP Images.

WEBSITES

Due to the changing nature of Internet links, Rosen Publishing has developed an online list of websites related to the subject of this book. This site is updated regularly. Please use this link to access the list: www.powerkidslinks.com/SOGI/equality